My Brain Needs
Glasses

For their colorful imagination
and boundless creativity,
a very special thank you to:

Gabriel, Maxime, Alexandre, Samuel,

Frédérique, Cathou, Jordanne, Anne-Marie,

Hugo, Charles-Olivier, Ève-Marie, Amélie,

Camille, Patricia, Tristan, Léandre, Ariane, Éliane, Sophie,

Philippe, Guillaume, Katherine, William, Vincent, Félix,

Marie-Hélène, Louis-Charles, Laurie, Marie-Philippe,

Gabrielle, Virginie, Jasmine, Roxanne, Louis, Jérémie,

Véronique, Gabrielle, Antoine, Blanche, Alexia, Jolan,

Laurence, Antoine, Xavier, Carole Anne, Léonie,

Lydiane, Charles-Éric, Philippe, KellyAnn

and the teachers at École Les Sources.

Dr. Annick Vincent

My Brain Needs Needs Glasses

ADHD explained to kids

4th edition

JUNIPER PUBLISHING

Project Editor: Marianne Prairie
Graphic Design: Christine Hébert
Translation: Paul de Tourreil
Editing and revision: Alison Ramsey
Proofreading: Robert Ronald

Catalogage avant publication de Bibliothèque et
Archives nationales du Québec et Bibliothèque et
Archives Canada

Title: My brain needs glasses : ADHD explained to
kids / Annick Vincent.
Other titles: Mon cerveau a besoin de lunettes.
English
Names: Vincent, Annick, 1965- author.
Description: 4th edition. | Translation of: Mon cer-
veau a besoin de lunettes. | Includes bibliographical
references.
Identifiers: Canadiana (print) 2022001292X
| Canadiana (ebook) 20220012938
| ISBN 9781988002941
| ISBN 9781988002958 (EPUB)
Subjects: LCSH: Attention-deficit hyperactivity
disorder—Juvenile literature.
Classification: LCC RJ506.H9 V5513 2022
| DDC j618.92/8589—dc23

Follow us on the Web
Visit our website, sign on to our newsletter to stay
informed about new titles and online contests.
You'll also meet favorite authors and Les Éditions
de l'Homme's editorial team on our blogs.

EDITIONS-HOMME.COM
EDITIONS-JOUR.COM
EDITIONS-PETITHOMME.COM
EDITIONS-LAGRIFFE.COM
RECTOVERSO-EDITEUR.COM
QUEBEC-LIVRES.COM
EDITIONS-LASEMAINE.COM

09-22

Legal deposit: 2022
National Library of Québec
National Library of Canada

ISBN 978-1-988002-94-1

EXCLUSIVE DISTRIBUTOR:

For Canada and the United States:
Simon & Schuster Canada
166 King Street East, Suite 300
Toronto, ON M5A 1J3
phone: (647) 427-8882
        1-800-387-0446
Fax: (647) 430-9446
simonandschuster.ca

Conseil des arts   Canada Council
du Canada   for the Arts

We gratefully acknowledge the support of the Canada
Council for the Arts for its publishing program.

Financé par le gouvernement du Canada
Funded by the Government of Canada   Canadä

We acknowledge the financial support of the
Government of Canada through the Canada Book
Fund for our publishing activities.

Preface

My Brain Needs Glasses is a must-have tool for creating dialogue with children who have ADHD (Attention Deficit Hyperactivity Disorder) and those around them. Relying on the latest scientific discoveries, this book is a treasure trove of information, and – *finally!* – it's addressed directly to kids. What a relief for children to feel that they can be understood by the people in their lives. Helping a child find strategies to manage ADHD means giving them wings so they can let their full potential take flight.

Be sure to share this gem of a book with those who spend time with your child from day to day! Teachers, coaches, babysitters, grandparents, sisters, brothers and children in the neighborhood – all of them can benefit from this essential tool kit. Embracing the uniqueness of these children and opening up pathways for them to express their spontaneity, energy and amazing creativity will help them capitalize on their strengths and become adults with fulfilling lives who will enrich our world.

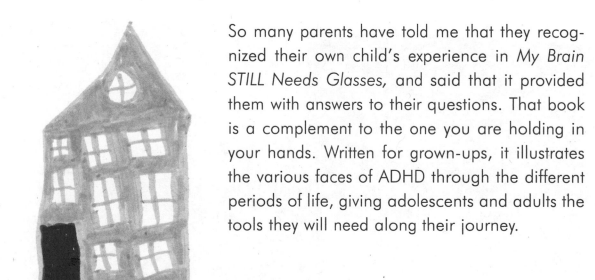

So many parents have told me that they recognized their own child's experience in *My Brain STILL Needs Glasses,* and said that it provided them with answers to their questions. That book is a complement to the one you are holding in your hands. Written for grown-ups, it illustrates the various faces of ADHD through the different periods of life, giving adolescents and adults the tools they will need along their journey.

Having access to tools like this would certainly have made my own life a lot easier: I've had to deal with ADHD on a daily basis for as long as I can remember. Today I approach it as a doctor, but also as the mother of three wonderful children who, despite the challenges presented by ADHD, have become successful and fulfilled adults. I'm proud of our differences and of all that we've accomplished!

And so, a gigantic thank you to the author. Generous and dedicated, Dr. Annick Vincent has helped share information all over the world for years now. An ambassador for ADHD awareness and a passionate doctor with contagious enthusiasm, she does an expert job of sharing her impressive knowledge with us.

Dr. Suzanne Pelletier
Pediatrician

Preface

ADHD and mood and anxiety disorders share some similarities in terms of research and clinical experience. For diagnosis and therapy, the optimal approach requires taking various elements into account, and the change has to start with the persons affected by the condition and their families. To thrive, they must have access to proven effective treatment and to skilled professionals, in a timely manner. Diagnosing ADHD and implementing the right strategies requires taking a global approach, with multiple modes of intervention. It often means having a multidisciplinary team (specialists and family doctors, along with teachers and other health care professionals). This book serves as a tool kit for all of them: not only for young people and their families but also for everyone else in their lives and those who play supporting roles. Dr. Annick Vincent, a dedicated psychiatrist and excellent spokesperson for ADHD awareness, shares what science tells us about ADHD and strategies for coping with the condition – all in a colorful format that's accessible to all.

When I was training in general medicine, ADHD was not well represented in the curriculum. Like many, I had to learn about it in the field. When I replaced a retired pediatrician who had been treating children with severe problems from five different schools, Dr. Vincent was a great help to me. Thanks to her teachings and her support, both scientific and emotional, our team was able to help and support schools and families. She has been a mentor and an instructor, always ready to help my colleagues and me in our work. Since she released the wonderful tools that are *My Brain Needs Glasses* and *My Brain STILL Needs Glasses*, our patients — children, adolescents and adults alike — have compared their treatment to glasses: "Doctor, I need to adjust my glasses!" The illustrated explanations and strategies presented have helped us support and motivate people and create stronger partnerships. Finally, we can speak the same language and move forward together.

I am happy to see the arrival of this new and fully updated edition, which uses the same rigor and accessible language and has the same goal: to build a partnership between the medical community and the rest of the world.

Thank you, Annick, my friend, for everything you have given us with your gift for communication, your creativity and your heart!

Dr. Christiane Laberge
Family Physician

A message to families living with ADHD

Deep down, I always knew I was a superhero, but reading this book confirmed it. Just like Superman, I didn't know my own strength at first. Now I know that I can accomplish extraordinary feats, that I can "fly" safely, because I have learned to control and understand the strength that lies within me.

It is precisely the lack of understanding of ADHD, by us and by those around us, that makes everyday life more complicated. I remember the first time I read this book (and yes, I have reread it — with each of my children!). If you only knew how good it felt to finally understand what had been so hard for me when I was young, to realize that I wasn't just an "annoying little pest"! As she was reading the book, my daughter said to me, "Daddy, we're the same!" I was so proud of her. And I was able to accompany her effectively, because now I can explain what is happening to us, and help her understand that our brains need glasses!

I hope that this book will bring you the same sense of serenity that it brought me. May it shine a new light and make a difference in your family, as it did in mine. Accepting and understanding ADHD is the starting point for many amazing family adventures!

You are not alone: yes, there are other people like you and me.

I actually need real glasses now, but that's because I'm 46. When I add in the ADHD, it's like I've got bifocals!

Phil

Comedian, President of the Fondation Philippe Laprise

Comments from adults who grew up with ADHD

When I was little, people called me names like scatter-brain and chatterbox. Despite my parents' help, it was very hard for me to study. I was unfocused, impulsive and slow. I had trouble getting organized. People thought I was lazy. I felt inferior and was always worried about failing in school. But in spite of everything, I loved to learn.

My own childhood and Tom's are separated by 34 years. If I had been as lucky as him, I would have been more successful in school and had a more rewarding social life, a career I enjoyed and, consequently, better self-esteem.

Today I understand myself, I'm proud of who I am, I have strategies I rely on and I take care of myself. My love of learning remains, but now I'm more enthusiastic than ever before. I'm better equipped, and life seems to hold a lot more promise.

As a child, I was like Tom. School was a nightmare that gave me stomachaches. Still, thanks to my parents' support and my somewhat creative and perfectionist side, I made it all the way to university. However, I always handed in my assignments late and filled with errors caused by distraction. The result: I was constantly stressed and convinced that the engine I had to rely on – my brain – was not up to the task.

Since then, I learned what the trouble really was. Now I wear the "glasses" I need, and I no longer feel like I'm lost in a maze. I know how my engine works and I'm cruising confidently down the highway. I'm successful in my work and proud of what I've accomplished. My son is now facing the same problems I faced. I don't want him to go through the same sort of doubt and uncertainty that cast a shadow over my own childhood.

Fortunately, he is surrounded by people who understand the nature of his difficulties. With the "glasses" he needs, he's doing great. He uses helpful tips and techniques, he concentrates better and he retains the information he learns in class. Best of all, he has better self-esteem.

My only regret today is that I didn't wear "glasses" when I was Tom's age. How lucky he is!

Carole

✿ Acknowledgments

A very special thank-you to the adults and children affected by ADHD who, by sharing their experiences and their strategies for adapting to this neurological disorder, have helped us better understand their difficulties and intervene with more suitable treatments. Thank you to the parents, teachers, health professionals and researchers for their continuous efforts to better grasp the complexity of this disorder and to find personalized treatments.

A thank-you from the bottom of my heart to all those who helped develop this book, from near or far: my family and friends, my patients and colleagues and the students, parents and the staff at École Les Sources. Your contributions, support and enthusiasm for this project have allowed it to take shape and to become what it is today.

Thank you also to the readers – with hopes that your curiosity and interest in better understanding ADHD is contagious. Happy reading!

Dr. Annick Vincent
Psychiatrist

HELLO, my name's Tom. I'm
8 years old and I'm in grade 3.
This is my family. I go to school.
These are my friends and
my teacher.

I'm creative, excitable, funny
and I have a big heart.

Wait! Don't
start without
me!

I'll tell you a secret about me:
Ever since I was little, I've had a
tendency to get "spaced out."

My ideas jump around like popcorn. It's hard to keep my concentration when **my thoughts are banging around in my head like bumper cars.** My brain seems to have a hard time distinguishing between what I see, hear and think. My attention wanders to anything happening around me.

I try hard, but I'm easily distracted, and I still make careless mistakes – even when I go over my work, I miss items! I forget things – so many things! I've even handed in a test and forgotten to fill in a section. I forget my lunch box, my notebook, my gym bag…

So many times my parents have had to bring me something I forgot to take to school – or had to go back to school to get something I left there. They say I'd make a great astronaut, because I'm always spacing out – and they need a spaceship to keep up with me. So much time is wasted on finding things I lose and forget!

"Where did my hat go?"

I try hard, but the problem is too big for me. When I read, I have to start over again and again, because I forget all the details.

I don't notice time passing,
and I often end up being late.
Sometimes my brain has a
hard time getting started,
and sometimes it seems to
be racing at top speed – but
not always in the right direction.

**People call me a
weather vane**
because I'm always turning
every which way. It's hard
to start a project, and
also to finish it: I lose my
focus and get scattered.
It's really frustrating:
no matter how hard I try,
I can't get organized 👀.

Sometimes it really bothers me – sometimes it even makes me angry. One day, another kid said that I must be stupid or lazy. That really hurt.

I wish someone could help me control the storm of thoughts in my head. I'm so lucky that my parents and my teacher give me support! I don't do it on purpose…

It feels like the bandleader in my brain doesn't know which direction to go.

I can't even keep up with myself sometimes. When I'm really interested and passionate about something, when I'm excited about a project or scrambling at the last minute, I can be super effective. If you think of it like a race, I'm an expert at sprinting!

But paying attention for long periods of time — that's another story. And it's even worse when the subject doesn't interest me or when I have to sit without moving.

I feel like no one notices it when I'm "lost in space." But one thing everyone notices is that I'm restless. Fidgeting is my specialty! I'm always moving. I run and climb like I'm in the Olympics.

My parents say that I was a real hurricane when I was little. Even as a baby, I couldn't stay in one place. My mother says that I learned to run before I learned to walk – she always laughs about it.

I need things to HAPPEN! Otherwise, I just drift into space. Waiting is torture for me – I get really grumpy if I have to wait too long.

My teacher has given me lots of warnings because I talk in class. Even if the subject is interesting to me, **I can't sit still in my chair – I move around, draw pictures, get up and talk nonstop.** When I have an idea, I have to say it right away – otherwise I'll forget it! This bothers my friends, but it's really hard for me to control.

Most of the time, I'm very funny and imaginative. My friends laugh when I clown around. I have a lot of good ideas. I'm known for my ability to find original solutions when problems arise. I have plenty of projects going on all the time. But I don't have enough brakes. In the schoolyard, I run all over the place. Sometimes I get warnings because I run into other kids when I'm zipping around.

Sometimes, I lose control. My emotions rise up like a big wave and I throw a fit... but it doesn't mean I'm mean!

My body and my thoughts
are in constant motion
from morning until night.

It's like the batteries in my brain are
overcharged. It's tiring in the long run.
Some evenings, I can't even get to sleep.
I move around nonstop. Lots of ideas race
through my head. I want to sleep,
but I just can't do it.

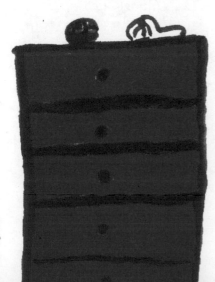

My parents get totally exhausted. They've tried reading stories, giving me massages, even making threats, but nothing works. But then in the morning, it's hard for me to get going. My mom and dad sometimes have to drag me out of bed…

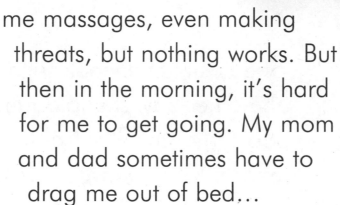

Being distracted and fidgety is sometimes a dangerous mixture. I can be pretty clumsy. **No matter how much I try, I injure myself often and make messes.**

My grandma says that my mom was just like me when she was little, but maybe less fidgety. She daydreamed all the time, got lost in her thoughts, and even though she didn't run all the time like me, she was clumsy. She got new cuts and bruises every day.

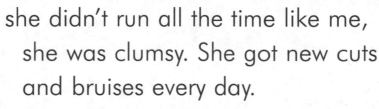

She hasn't changed much, either. Just the other day, she told me that looking at me was like looking in a mirror. Even today, her mind is always wandering, and then she has to run around at the last minute; she's often late and totally disorganized. Want proof? Just look at her office!

Mom's office

Last year, my teacher, who had seen other kids with similar problems, told my parents that we should see a special doctor to find out what was happening to me.

So we went to see a doctor. He met with my parents and found out what my teachers had seen. I like him. He talks to me, not just to my parents. **He told us that he thought I had Attention-Deficit/Hyperactivity Disorder, or ADHD.**

ADHD??? Albino Dinosaur with Hiccup Distress!!!

Hic!
Hic!
Hic!

It's a problem that happens when the brain has a hard time focusing and slowing things down when it should.

When the brain sends messages, it transmits them to different areas using a network of wires, called neurons. The **information moves along pathways that are kind of like highways;** these highways have intersections and connect with other roads.

Normally, the messages know where to go. Neurotransmitters – they're sort of like traffic police – make sure that they start and stop at the right times, and that they yield to others when they should.

ADHD CRITERIA

To make a diagnosis of ADHD, all the following characteristics should be present, whatever the age of the person being assessed:

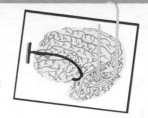

ADHD symptoms:

- ☒ have been present since early childhood. In adolescents and adults, one should be able to trace symptoms of inattention or hyperactivity-impulsivity before or by the age of 12
- ☒ have persisted for at least six months
- ☒ appear in at least two different settings (e.g., home, school, work)
- ☒ have led to significant functional impairment in various spheres of daily life (social, academic or professional)
- ☒ are not better explained by another psychiatric, medical or psychosocial condition and do not correspond to the normal level of development for the person's age

A minimum of symptoms in the following list should be observable:

- ☐ 16 years and under: AT LEAST six out of the nine symptoms of inattention and/or hyperactivity-impulsivity
- ☐ 17 years and over: AT LEAST five out of the nine symptoms of inattention and/or hyperactivity-impulsivity

1. Inattention / The person:

- ☐ has difficulty paying attention to details and makes careless mistakes
- ☐ has difficulty sustaining attention
- ☐ seems not to be listening when being spoken to directly
- ☐ doesn't follow instructions or finish tasks (without this being oppositional behavior)
- ☐ has difficulty planning and organizing work or activities
- ☐ avoids, postpones or performs reluctantly tasks that require sustained mental effort
- ☐ loses objects necessary for their work or activities
- ☐ is easily distracted by external stimuli or his or her own thoughts
- ☐ frequently forgets things in daily life

2. Hyperactivity/impulsivity
Motor hyperactivity

The person:

- ☐ often fidgets with hands and feet or squirms in chair
- ☐ often gets up in situations where one should remain sitting
- ☐ runs around and climbs a lot (with increasing age: feeling of restlessness or fidgetiness)
- ☐ has a hard time keeping still at school, work or in recreational activities
- ☐ is often excited or worked up
- ☐ often talks too much

Impulsivity / The person:

- ☐ answers questions before they are finished
- ☐ has difficulty waiting their turn
- ☐ often interrupts or intrudes upon others

Presentations of ADHD

Combined ADHD = meets criteria 1 and 2 (the most common form).

ADHD with predominant inattention = only meets criteria 1.

ADHD with predominant hyperactivity = only meets criteria 2.

Adapted from *Diagnostic and Statistical Manual of Mental Disorders*, Fifth Edition (DSM-5), American Psychiatric Association, Washington DC, 2013.

The doctor explained to us that **ADHD** is a neurological disorder caused by a problem with the brain's information highways. When the traffic police don't do their job well (for example, if they are asleep or they aren't seeing properly), traffic doesn't move properly, and things get really messed up. When that happens, your thoughts get all mixed up and bump into each other.

★ **TIP** ★

EVERYTHING HAS ITS PLACE! I'm learning to organize my environment really well. I always remember that if I don't see something, my brain will probably forget it exists. I separate my stuff into transparent boxes, drawers and baskets, and I label them. Then it's easier to find things later! I hang my clothes on hooks - if I don't, I tend to leave things lying around everywhere.

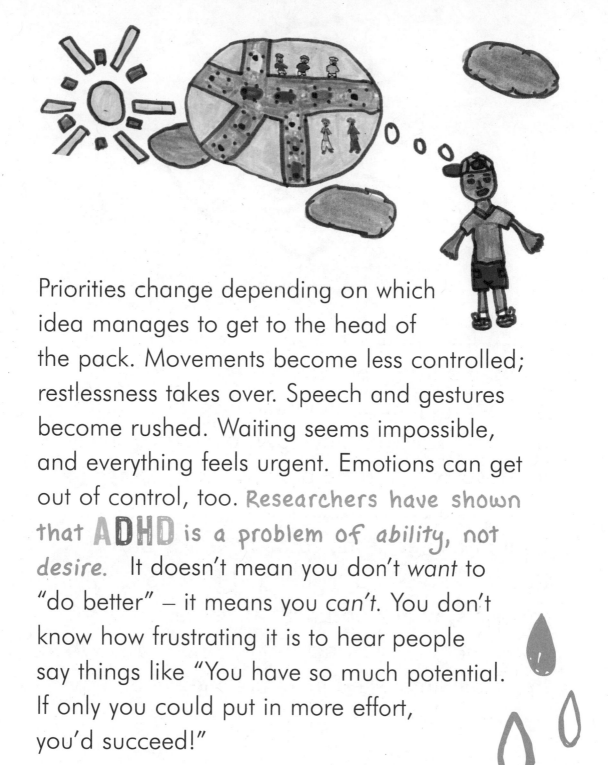

Priorities change depending on which idea manages to get to the head of the pack. Movements become less controlled; restlessness takes over. Speech and gestures become rushed. Waiting seems impossible, and everything feels urgent. Emotions can get out of control, too. Researchers have shown that ADHD is a problem of *ability*, not *desire*. It doesn't mean you don't *want* to "do better" — it means you *can't*. You don't know how frustrating it is to hear people say things like "You have so much potential. If only you could put in more effort, you'd succeed!"

When the brain wants to concentrate on one thing, the traffic police have to get to work and keep other commands (thoughts, words and actions) from getting in their way. Their job is to put up road blocks. But my ADHD makes the commands all show up in the control center at the same time. My brain doesn't know what command to follow. My thoughts, words and actions get less coordinated, and I act more impulsively. When I'm really interested in something, when I'm hyper-stimulated or when I try really hard, I can activate the traffic police somewhat, but not always enough or for long. And it takes so much energy!

TIP

MAKING REMINDERS HELPS A LOT.
I've been finding tricks to help me remember important information. I write down or draw the things I don't want to forget on a notepad, or I put notes up on my bulletin board.

There are tips and medication that can help me lessen the intensity and consequences of **ADHD**. They stimulate certain regions in my brain so that I can better concentrate, a little like **glasses for the brain.**

I've learned that the more interested and motivated I am and the more I enjoy doing something, the more active my traffic police becomes. And that's exactly what ADHD medication does! That means that understanding myself, what I love, finding ways to be motivated and focusing on my strengths can help me grow into an ADHD champion!

★ TIP ★

MY BRAIN IS A REAL SPRINTER! THERE ARE WAYS I CAN AVOID LOSING MY FOCUS. EVERY TIME I'M FACED WITH A TASK, I TAKE THE FOLLOWING STEPS:

1) I break down the task into shorter steps.

2) I do the most important steps first.

3) I give myself reasonable deadlines and I make sure to meet them.

4) I congratulate myself when I succeed, and I give myself rewards when I can (for example, more time for an activity I like).

The doctor told us that **ADHD** is often hereditary. It's transmitted in our genes, which come from our parents, the same as the color of our eyes or our hair. Some children develop the condition because their brain was injured when they were little (for example, because they were premature or they had an infection, like meningitis). **ADHD** affects boys and girls alike.

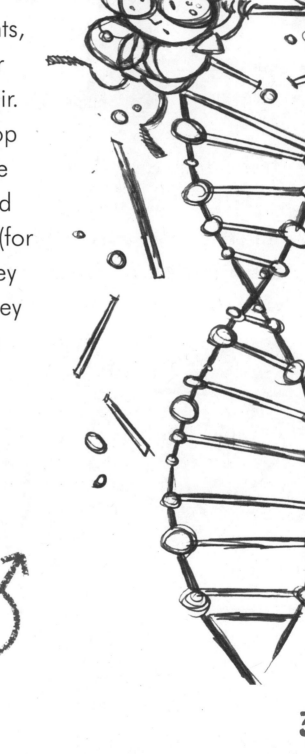

In my immediate family, my mother and I have **ADHD**. Most of the time, children and adults living with **ADHD** have a combination of behaviors: 'inattentive • fidgety • impulsive'

The doctor explained to us that hyperactivity of movement and speech is only the visible part of ADHD. Just like the tip of an iceberg, it's the part we can see easily, but we don't realize that there is so much more under the surface!

Our brain's ability to focus is influenced by many things, including our mood, motivation and energy. In ADHD, hyperactivity also affects our thoughts, which explains why it's so hard for us to pay attention! It takes a good detective to figure out that ADHD is the cause when the lack of A (attention) is the only sign of the H (hyperactivity)! In this case, it is not our bodies that are buzzing, but our thoughts!

When we live with **ADHD**, our mind is drawn to everything we hear or see. Even our own ideas take us elsewhere! Our thoughts wander and stray down many different paths. That squirrel we spot out of the corner of our eye takes us somewhere else, and then — poof! — we realize we've lost the thread: we're not in the right place anymore and we have to somehow find our way back!

My mom was a grown-up when she learned that her mistakes due to not paying attention, trouble concentrating, forgetfulness and general "scatterbrain" were signs of **ADHD**. She was often tired, but didn't know why. The doctor explained that it takes a lot of "brain fuel" to try to stay focused through such a whirlwind!

My parents were surprised to learn that almost half of children with ADHD will continue to have some related problems as they grow up, and even as adults. That means that even though my mother is all grown up, her brain may still need glasses!

ADHD can cause difficulties at school (or at work for adults), at home and with friends. So it's important to know how your brain works so you can find strategies to live with it!

If **ADHD** isn't treated, kids may have so much trouble at school that they drop out. Others may become so impulsive that they can't even follow instructions. Kids with **ADHD** may hurt themselves or have accidents. On the other hand, having lots of original ideas and projects is quite an advantage when you channel it well. There are plenty of star athletes and CEOs who have **ADHD** and have learned to master it.

It was hard when I first learned that I had this problem. I felt like I was different from my friends. But at the same time, I was happy to finally learn what was happening to me.

I understood that I wasn't stupid, like that boy said. My brain works differently, that's all!

I explained to my friends that I'm just made this way! I'm kind of like my friend Julia. She couldn't see the board well and had to squint her eyes all the time, until finally she got glasses. The difference is that no one sees my glasses!

★ **TIP** ★

TIDAL WAVE OF EMOTIONS RISING UP?
I often take little breaks to relax and unwind. When my emotions get too strong, I focus on my breathing to calm down. Knowing what is going on inside me helps me to discover why I'm feeling the way I do. It always feels better to take a step back instead of letting myself be overwhelmed by emotions.

You know, a lot of people — like me — are able to function with ADHD, but it takes lots of effort.

But some people don't succeed as well as they could. Some get discouraged, are hard on themselves and get more and more stressed out.

⭐ **TIP** ⭐

"KNOW YOURSELF!"
I watch myself and try to figure out which conditions I work best in. Silence? With soft music? While doodling?

I was lucky to learn about my problems early and to find solutions for them. **Now I have glasses for my brain — and they look great on me!**

⭐ **TIP** ⭐

HAVING A ROUTINE HAS ITS BENEFITS!
I set up a routine for my daily life and I stick to it. This helps me to stay organized, remember things better and feel more in control.

Hmm... very interesting!

ADHD

The first step is learning what **ADHD** is. My parents and I have read books about it and we've even found some good sites on the Internet.

But be careful! You have to use common sense while reading about **ADHD**, and don't believe everything that is written. My parents helped me realize that it's worth taking the time to check the sources for the information you find…to be sure that what you're reading is true.

★ **TIP** ★

I'M GETTING ORGANIZED! Color codes, lists, memos, calendars and note cards all help me to remember important tasks. It's a good way for me to get organized more effectively.

My parents, my teacher and I have learned to work as a team so that I stay organized. They're like my coaches. They help me by encouraging me to get started, stay interested and keep my concentration. When I get tangled, they remind me what the instructions are. They also help me to use my calendar. I discovered that by using notes and putting everything in its place, I get less confused.

I learned to break down tasks into smaller parts and to set a specific time on my calendar to complete them. That means I get to set my own pace for the whole task.

I can do short sprints and take breaks. That means I'm less exhausted and I finish on time, and my efforts pay off in my work!

I've learned to move around without disturbing people much, so I can keep my concentration – it's a real challenge! I play sports to channel my energy, and I try to control myself when I'm about to interrupt someone. It's hard and it takes a lot of energy.

When I stop using these strategies, I lose my concentration. It's as though my brain has stopped using its glasses.

Waste my time? No way! I've equipped myself with devices for measuring time: a watch, an alarm clock, an hourglass...

 Check out my super-watch. I use it to make sure I start or finish on time. I can make the alarm go off to start something or to finish on time.

 I still have moments when I can't control my ideas and actions.
Big waves of emotion still pop up on the horizon at times. I try to use self-control, but it's a big job every day. Whatever happens, crying or getting mad is not the answer.

The doctor explained to us that in many cases, medicine is needed to help a brain with **ADHD** work better.

These medicines work like tiny glasses inside the body, and they directly improve how the traffic police work.

The goal is that medicine will improve my brain's ability to focus so I can function to my best potential. My doctor told me that these are the medicine's **primary effects**.

Some of these medicines have only short-term effects. If so, you need to take them more than once a day. Other medicines last for many hours, sometimes all day long, so you only have to take them once a day. You need to find the right type and the right dose, because everyone is different. We have to visit our doctor regularly, because our doctor is the person who helps us find the right treatment.

For me, we had to make adjustments for three months to get it right. For my mom, it took longer, because the first medicine that she tried didn't help her.

Sometimes the medicines produce effects that we don't want. These are called secondary effects, or side effects. Some people may lose their appetite, for instance. If so, they may need to take smaller portions and eat more often.

ZZZZ

If a medicine stimulates your brain too much, you may have difficulty falling asleep. My doctor warned me that if the dose is too strong for me, I may feel too hyper or very grumpy. Sometimes, you can even become so focused on something that you don't notice the things that are going on around you. That's why people sometimes say they feel like a zombie. If that happens, you need to talk to your doctor so the treatment can be adjusted.

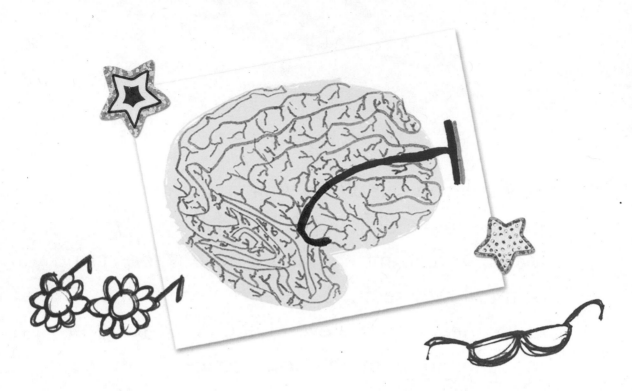

The goal is to have as many positive effects as possible, and as few negative effects! Once you find the right pair of glasses, the **ADHD** symptoms will be reduced – but they won't disappear.

Strategies for coping with **ADHD** are easier to apply when your brain is well fed and rested.

MEDICINES AREN'T MAGIC!

Glasses for the eyes help us see letters better, and that helps us read! For people with 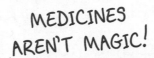, glasses for the brain help you concentrate more... but they don't actually do the things you need to do yourself!

When you're in a good mood and more attentive, your tasks are also easier to finish. When you're less impulsive, you have time to think things over before you act — that means you will have fewer conflicts with others. It's easier at home, with friends and at school. **When you see that your efforts are helping, you feel less frustrated and more satisfied.** Succeeding makes you feel proud and happier in your everyday life. These are the real primary effects of treatment.

Not everyone who has **ADHD** needs medicine. I have friends who also have **ADHD**, and the strategies that are good for them aren't necessarily good for me.

I think that the important thing is to know that my brain needs glasses and to use all the glasses that suit me. My parents and my teacher help me get organized. They believe in me and support me, and that makes a huge difference!

I do my best to apply myself, and my medicine makes it easier for the traffic police in my brain to do their work.

It still bothers me when people ask questions about **ADHD**. But most of all I don't like it when people don't understand or when they make fun of me. Sometimes it's hard... My friend Kelly Ann is in grade 1. She has **ADHD**, too. She has so much H – hyperactivity – that she can't sit still. She can't pay attention for long enough to learn in class.

Other kids say she's rough and sometimes annoying. But if they took the time to get to know her, they'd see that she's kind and gentle. It's frustrating. If they could see the blizzard of thoughts swirling around in her head, they would understand. Look, even her pencil is always on the go!

before

after

Can you tell the difference between the two drawings, since she found the right pair of glasses for her brain? The detail, the colors— wow! What an artist! **Now she's able to choose where to put her attention and show how creative she is.**

At the beginning, I thought I was the only one with **ADHD**. But my doctor told me that about one in 20 kids has it. That means that at my school there's probably one kid in every class who is affected.

That also means that in a movie theater that seats 200 people, about 10 people have ADHD. And in a city with 200,000 residents, it would be 10,000 people!

★ **TIP** ★

UNIQUE, DIFFERENT AND PROUD!

• I surround myself with positive people who help me.

• I focus on my accomplishments.

• I'm proud of who I am and what I do.

So, there are lots of people who have the same problem as me! Luckily, they can find solutions that work for them.

And you? Are you living with **ADHD**? If not, you might know other children, adolescents or adults who are. I hope that my story will help you to understand them better.

See you next time!
This is the end
of my journal —
time for me
to go and play!

Also available

MY BRAIN STILL NEEDS GLASSES
ADHD in adolescents and adults

Award by the Quebec Psychiatric Association

Vincent, A. (2023)
My Brain STILL Needs Glasses, (4th edition)
Juniper Publishing.

More than half of children with ADHD will still manifest symptoms in adulthood. That means they STILL need glasses and can benefit from knowing what tools are available to them.

With humorous insights and first-hand accounts, this book presents readers with scientific literature, the clinical symptoms of this neurological problem, and pharmacologic treatments for it. This practical guide also offers a wealth of effective tips and strategies specifically designed to help affected adults cope with ADHD in their daily lives.

Also available in French and Korean

Vincent, A. (2022). *Mon cerveau a besoin de lunettes: Le TDAH expliqué aux enfants*, Éditions de l'Homme.

Vincent, A. (2022). *Mon cerveau a ENCORE besoin de lunettes: Le TDAH chez les adolescents et les adultes*, Éditions de l'Homme

Resources and references

Visit the website about ADHD developed by the author, Dr. Annick Vincent, for other suggestions and tips.
attentiondeficit-info.com

 TIPS

TIPS, TRICKS, AND MORE TIPS...TO HELP YOU REMEMBER ALL
THE TIPS THAT I SUGGESTED IN MY JOURNAL, HERE'S A SUMMARY
THAT YOU CAN CUT OUT AND KEEP WITH YOU.

Everything has its place.

I've learned to organize my environment well, and I remember that for my
brain, the things I don't see don't even exist. I sort and put my stuff away in
labeled boxes, drawers and baskets. That means I can find things more
easily later! I hang my clothes on hooks, because otherwise I know I'll
probably leave them lying all over the place.

I make reminders.

I find ways to remember important information. I draw or write down
the things that I don't want to forget in a notebook, or put notes up on
a bulletin board.

My brain likes to sprint!
I find ways to avoid losing track of what I'm doing.

Every time I have to do a task, I take the following steps:

1. I break the task down into shorter steps.
2. I do the most important steps first.
3. I give myself reasonable deadlines and I stick to them.
4. I congratulate myself when I succeed and give myself rewards when
   I can (for example, more time for an activity that I love).

Tidal wave of emotions in sight?

I don't hesitate to take a little break to relax and unwind. When my emotions get too strong, I focus on my breathing to calm down. Knowing what
is going on inside me helps me to discover why I'm feeling the way I do.
I feel better taking a step back instead of letting myself be overwhelmed
by emotions.

Know my own self!

I watch myself and try to find the conditions in which I work best. In silence?
With soft music? While doodling?

Having a routine has its benefits!

I set up a routine for my daily life and I stick to it. This helps me stay organized and feel more in control.

I get organized!

Color codes, lists, memos, calendars and note cards all help me to remember important tasks. That way I can get organized more efficiently.

I move, you move, he moves...

I channel my need to move into sports and exercise. Then I feel less restless the rest of the time.

Waste my time? No way!

I use devices for measuring time: a watch, an alarm clock, an hourglass…

Need to solve a problem? No problem!

Here are some useful steps for solving problems:

1. Define the problem.
2. Make a list of possible solutions.
3. Choose a solution.
4. Apply the chosen solution.
5. Evaluate the impacts of that solution.
6. If necessary, redo the process by choosing another solution.

Unique, different and proud!

I surround myself with positive people who help me. I focus on my accomplishments. I'm proud of who I am and what I do!

A colorful life!

I find ways to add spice to my daily life: colors, music and humor are all wonderful ways to make my life more exciting and really great!